True
Remarkable
Occurrences

Madame de Maintenon and friends

True
Remarkable
Occurrences

Compiled & annotated by
John Train

Illustrations by Pierre Le-Tan
Preface by George Plimpton

Clarkson N. Potter, Inc., Publishers, New York
Distributed by Crown Publishers, Inc.

—Pierre Le-Tan

Published simultaneously in Canada by General Publishing Company Limited
First edition
Printed in the United States of America

Designed by Katy Homans
Type set in Monotype Dante by Michael & Winifred Bixler

Library of Congress Cataloging in Publication Data

Train, John.
  Remarkable occurrences.

  1. Anecdotes. I. Title.
PN6261.T66   808.88′2   78-16978
ISBN 0-517-53505-X
Second Printing, October, 1978

ACKNOWLEDGMENTS

Struggling poet (and friend) Christopher Logue, who edits a miscellany section in Private Eye, *provided valuable leads, as did Freling Foster's column in the old* Collier's. *Timothy Dickinson of* Harper's *and Nina Georges-Picot of the* Reader's Digest *were as usual generous with their time and learning. My thanks also to Hoyt Ammidon, John Bogert, Elena and Raymond Bonham-Carter, Ivan Brunk, Lord David Cecil, Bill Cole of the* Saturday Review, *Nicholas Comfort of the* Daily Telegraph, *Virgil Dugen, Alix Hornblower, and Terry Kay of the British Museum Library, James Michaels of* Forbes, *Patricia Polak, Richard Reade, Harry Tower, Maria Teresa Train, Judge Richard Wallach, and C.P.E. Wrangell; to my perceptive editor, Carol Southern, my assistant, Louisa Spencer, and particularly Francie, my wife.*

I gratefully acknowledge permission granted from Debrett's Peerage Limited to reproduce from The Big Shots: Edwardian Shooting Parties *by Jonathan Garnier Ruffer; to the Genealogical Publishing Company for permission to reproduce from* Kentucky Marriages, 1797–1865; *to Houghton Mifflin Company for permission to reproduce from* The Cecils of Hatfield House *by David Cecil (© 1973 by Lord David Cecil); and to J. B. Lippincott Company for permission to reproduce from* Stay of Execution *by Stewart Alsop (© 1973 by J. B. Lippincott Company).*

PREFACE

I have known the compiler of this volume for many years. He was the first managing editor of the literary magazine The Paris Review—*a position he held until one day he gently let me know he was moving on to other things by leaving a note in his* IN *box which read Do Not Put Anything In This Box.*

He is a slight figure with a long, quite melancholy face. It is a scholar's face, and yet I have seen it (in circumstances too complicated to go into) under a chauffeur's cap, a World War I steel helmet, a baseball cap, a Bedouin kefieh, and the headgear never seems inappropriate. He is a man of many categories. For example, he is one of the world's great skippers of stones. I have watched him at this practice . . . first, the careful selection of the proper stone, a stooped, slow inspection of the detritus along the seashore, and then, the choice made, a curious windmilling throwing style sending the stone dimpling its way out across the water toward the horizon. It is not enough to be able to do this with skill; he is an authority on hurling flat objects . . . and can provide a disquisition on George Washington skipping the silver dollar over the Delaware.

In more practical areas, my friend John Train has for years associated himself with the world of high finance and commerce. Here again, he has cast his net wide. There was a point shortly after he got out of college when the rumor swept the Paris cafés that he had been exporting live birds — some breed of finch, I seem to remember — across the Egyptian border in crates, hundreds of birds at a time. He was said to have "cornered" the finch market — which I suppose was reason enough to be involved — but then the price of finches had suddenly collapsed, leaving Train in a hotel room in Beirut with the now worthless finches creating such an uproar that the hotel guests were beginning to complain, pounding on the floor and walls. According to the legend, Train let his finches go, not out the window as one might suppose, but into the corridors where the birds spread out through the hotel and hopped about in merry clamor.

Some time back I thought to ask him about this, about the difficulty of taking such a vast number of birds across borders. I have heard two finches squabbling in their cage, which produces racket enough, and the thought of crates of finches . . . the border guards . . . the corner of the tarpaulin lifted . . . the query, "What is this, please?". . .

Before I could go further, Train produced a sharp cluck of dismay. He said he had indeed purchased a bird in Tel Aviv, but it was a single specimen with a key in its back, a toy bird he thought a friend of his in the toy business in London might be interested to see. He seemed irked that the truth had gotten so out of hand.

This is typical of the Train ethic — he could never become a party to a fabrication, even to a tall tale of considerable charm (what is more romantic than to have the reputation of being an international finch speculator?). Being such a stickler for the facts, with a horror of the inaccurate, Train is the quintessential compiler of such a volume as Remarkable Occurrences. A less scrupulous encyclopedist would give in to temptation, embroidering his entries to make them more ludicrous and hilarious. Or he would tend to slip an "occurrence" into the text, which while stupendous in effect, could not be verified as having actually happened.

Here is an example of the care taken with an "occurrence" which crossed Train's desk. "A Baltimore plant tried piping in boogie-woogie music for the workers. Seventy-one of them had to receive psychiatric treatment at Johns Hopkins Hospital." Since the item had been accredited by Freling Foster, the distinguished collector of squibs for Collier's Magazine, the authenticity of this candidate for inclusion seemed assured. But when Train's researchers checked with the psychiatric staff at Johns Hopkins (with "extremely elderly psychiatrists who go back a long, long way") the doctors said they had never heard of the practice. Accordingly, if with regret, the item was dropped.

So was an episode involving the Atlanta Symphony Orchestra. The report reaching Train (which was reported in Christopher Logue's department "True Stories" in the English periodical Private Eye) described a performance of the Tchaikovsky 1812 Overture during which the cannon-device backstage performed with such vigor that the automatic fire-extinguishing system in the concert hall was set off, not only enveloping the startled audience with foam, but bringing a helmeted brigade of firemen hurrying into the hall and, with axes at the ready, charging into a dazed audience still trying to cope with the foam.

Unfortunately, this splendid, visually absorbing drama turned out to be what the Train staff called a "gross exaggeration." True, the cannon-device had alerted the fire department, but the foam, and the axes at the ready, and the audience-firemen confrontation all proved to be embellishments by Mr. Logue, a distinguished English poet. "Poetic License" is not allowed to infect these pages!

That does not mean, however, that one's imagination cannot abound in relish of each of these "occurrences." The sparseness of the prose, just the bare bones of the episode, is exactly correct. it allows the reader to provide his own mental elaboration, and, in many cases, to speculate on "what happened then?"

After reading the episode "Lovers Cut Free from Embrace" (20) one can enjoy an idle moment imagining what the unfortunate woman did eventually say to her husband about his car.

Or, wonder if the railroad officials ever did get the Bishop of Exeter to his confirmation ceremony (48) and, if so, how they managed to find out where he was going.

Or, did Hans and Erna W. buy another poodle after what happened in Hong Kong (60) and what did they tell their friends back in Zurich?

Or, what did King Gustavus II Adolphus of Sweden say to his ship's designer after the Vasa sank at its launching?(23)

Now, has Mr. Train himself been involved in "Remarkable Occurrences?" He has indeed. While President of *the* Harvard Lampoon *he led a band of undergraduates costumed as British soldiers up to the Lexington Common and into a ceremony at which the Governor of Massachusetts was about to address a crowd of 3,000 or so. The shebang was being held to honor Patriot's Day, the anniversary of the day Paul Revere rode around the countryside shouting "The British are coming!" A very hallowed day in the Commonwealth to be sure. To our astonishment (I was one of the soldiers, carrying a fake wooden musket), Train led our band up onto the dais where he snatched the microphone away from the governor and called into it: "This is an unlawful assembly! You will all disperse to your homes!" The enormous crowd stared at him dumbly. The governor stood to one side with a faint smile on his face; perhaps he thought our appearance had to do with the panoply of the day. Then came what I would judge a "Remarkable Occurrence." Train — where most mortals would have fled not knowing what to do next — leaned forward and delivered himself of a long, impassioned defense of the Stamp Act. What's more, it made a great deal of sense. Why, if Train had been around in 1765 the colonies might have mumbled a bit, but they would have calmed down and we all might have been a little more like John Train. One could hardly do better.*

— George Plimpton

CONTENTS

Une jeune mère allaitait un serpent

INTRODUCTION

I have always had a weakness for curious episodes, what the French call faits divers. *In graduate school I sometimes included in my notes the literary anecdotes recounted by the lecturers. Several of the episodes in this book come from that time. European newspapers like them, and while living abroad I collected a number.*

My takeoff point in the bizarre occurrences business probably came in Toulouse, in 1952, en route from Spain to Italy. While having breakfast in a café, I read in the local paper—the Dépêche, *I think—under the headline* Une Jeune Mère Allaitait un Serpent (*"Young Mother Suckles Snake"), an account of an episode in Trastevere, a poor quarter of Rome. It seemed that a woman sitting in the open had fallen asleep while nursing her baby. A snake had appeared and taken the baby's place, had silenced the infant's cries by waving its tail to distract it . . . and so on.*

I showed this story with some enthusiasm to the waiter, who in the jaded manner of garçons de café *everywhere, particularly early in the morning, seemed unimpressed. "Ah, ça, vous savez, les ritales . . ."* he said, and wandered off, shrugging vaguely. Unsatisfied by this response, I sliced the story out of the paper and put it in my pocket. On reaching Florence, I tried it again on my aunt. "Si, si,*

*"*Wops . . .*"

13

di fatti," *she said, "It was in the* Nazione *and the* Corriere. *In the Italian papers they ended by saying, 'This kind of thing has been happening* all too frequently *of late in Trastevere!'"*

I felt better, and stowed the clipping in my billfold, where in time it was joined by others picked up along the way in travels or from reading. From this period came "Walking Iron Mine Finally Collapses," included in the present volume. As the collection grew, I began noting discoveries in my pocket appointment books. Finally in 1977 I exhumed my old notes and transcribed what seemed like the best, together with others looked up in various places or that have come in from correspondents.

Suggestions for a subsequent edition, or corrections, are very welcome indeed, and can be mailed to Box 157, R.D. 2, Bedford, New York. Documentation is important.

To illustrate the importance of verification, I might mention the "snake in the Christmas tree" archetype. Mr. David Binger, a close observer of conditions in the Bedford area, told me recently of a friend of his who had a neighbor who had bought a Christmas tree and taken it home with its roots wrapped in burlap. While he took a bath his wife started to cut open the burlap wrapping. Suddenly, a snake slid out from the tangle of roots. She shrieked. The husband dashed downstairs, naked and dripping. His wife excitedly told him about the snake. He snatched up a poker and peered at the base of the tree. The family retriever, intrigued, stuck his cold nose into the man's behind. The terrified man crashed into the wall, sustaining a concussion. An ambu-

lance was called. When the stretcher-bearers heard what had happened, they laughed so hard they dropped the victim, whose arm was broken.

I started checking this story, and pursued it upstream around Westchester County through six successive sources, each of whom assured me that it had actually happened to a friend of the person he had heard it from.

During this process, Mrs. Duncan Spencer sent in an account of a Connecticut woman who came home from shopping on a winter Saturday and noticed her husband on his back under the car performing some repair. The woman, who was of a frisky disposition, scooped up a handful of snow, adroitly zipped open his trousers, and shoveled it in. The supine form convulsed, cracking its head against the crankcase. Darkness loosened his limbs, as Homer says. The woman dashed into the house to phone the doctor. She encountered her actual husband, who mentioned that he had called a mechanic to fix the car. Again, the ambulance comes, the stretcher-bearer howls with laughter, the patient is let fall, his arm is broken.

I finally realized that both of these tales are almost certainly mutants of the London Times plumber story on page 59.

So one must nail down the exact origin. In the present text, anyway, the reader will observe that I've generally given citations for the contemporary episodes, and not always for the historical ones, most of which can be found in the standard sources.

—J. T.

Mrs Czermak's descent

ROMANTIC
ENTANGLEMEN

Mrs. Czermak's Descen

PRAGUE — Vera Czermak jumped out (
story window when she learned her h
betrayed her.

Mrs. Czermak is recovering in hospita.
ing on her husband, who was killed, the
Vecerni Pravha reported today. — *United I*

Speak for Yourself, Wong

TAIPEI — A young Taiwanese man has v
love letters to his girl friend over the past
trying to get her to marry him.

His persistence finally brought results.

A newspaper reported yesterday the gi
come engaged to the postman who faithfu
ered all the letters. — *United Press*

Good Form

Some months after obtaining his divorce, Walter Davis of London consulted a matrimonial bureau in the hope of finding a new companion, the *Settimana Enigmistica* of Milan reported in September, 1975.

Out of thousands of names, the bureau's computer selected that of his former wife, Ethel, who had consulted the same agency, and whom Mr. Davis obediently remarried.

Liebestodt

MARRIED: Moses Alexander, aged 93, to Mrs. Frances Tompkins, aged 105, in Bata, N. Y., on June 11, 1831.

They were both taken out of bed dead the following morning.*

Greek Drama

An Athenian took a taxi to his lady-love's house, letting himself in with a key she had given him.

After a while they were surprised *in flagrante* by the taxi driver, who had let himself in with his own key. It was his house. The lady was his wife.

*Kentucky Marriages, 1797–1865. Baltimore: Genealogical Publishing Company, 1966.

Here lies buried the bodies
of Moses Alexander
and Frances Tompkins
who departed this life
June the 11th 1831

Liebestodt

Lovers Cut Free from Embrace

LONDON — A tiny sports car leaves a lot to be desired as a midnight trysting spot, two secret lovers have learned.

Wedged into a two-seater, a near-naked man was suddenly immobilized by a slipped disc, trapping his woman companion beneath him, according to a doctor writing in a medical journal here.

The desperate woman tried to summon help by honking the horn with her foot. A doctor, ambulance driver, firemen, and a group of interested passersby* quickly surrounded the car in Regent's Park.

"The lady found herself trapped beneath 200 pounds of pain-racked, immobile man," said Dr. Brian Richards of Kent.

"To free the couple, firemen had to cut away the car frame," he said.

The distraught woman, helped out of the car and into a coat, sobbed: "How am I going to explain to my husband what has happened to his car?" — *Reuter*

Including women volunteer workers who arrived to serve tea, the London Sunday Mirror *reported.*

AFFAIRS OF STATE

Surtout Point de Zèle

Thomas Jefferson, speaking of the American minister to Spain: "I haven't heard from him in two years. If I don't hear from him next year, I will write him a letter."

Chops Populi

Victor Biaka-Boda, who represented the Ivory Coast in the French Senate,* set off on a tour of the hinterlands in January 1950 to let the people know where he stood on the issues, and to understand their concerns—one of which was apparently the food supply. His constituents ate him.

*His colleagues, according to an account in Time magazine in July 1951, remembered Biaka-Boda, a former witch doctor, as a "small, thin, worried-looking man."

The career of the Vasa

The Career of the Vasa

Gustavus II Adolphus, king of Sweden, troubled by Hapsburg pressure on the Baltic, commanded that the mightiest warship on any ocean be constructed as the flagship of his navy. Designed to carry 500 sailors and troops, she was named the *Vasa*, after his own dynasty.

Finally, her powerful armaments, her stout rigging, her splendid ornamentation, were complete.

On Sunday, August 10, 1628, Captain Söfring Hanson gave the order to sail. High court and military dignitaries were on board. A throng lined the Stockholm waterfront to admire the magnificent vessel and enjoy the soft light of the summer afternoon.

Warped along the quays of the Skeppsbron, her figurehead, a nobly carved and gilded lion, turned its grave face out into the bay. A gentle breeze from the heights of Söder filled the acres of white canvas.

The ship gained way slowly. She fired the two-gun salute of departure.

The wind picked up and the *Vasa* heeled, farther, farther . . .

Suddenly the sea poured into the open gunports, only a yard above the waterline.

With a deep, melancholy crashing and pounding as the munitions and stores shifted in the hold, the huge vessel heeled more sharply. The rail entered the water; the waves lapped over the deck. The hull slid into the depths. Masts and sails slowly vanished. Finally, the last pennant, bravely waving still, disappeared into the pale blue Baltic.*

Protocol

American Ambassador Joseph Hodges Choate was leaving an official reception in London, dressed in plain black, America having no diplomatic uniform. Another ambassador, mistaking him for a servant, briskly commanded, "Call me a cab!"

Choate gazed at him a moment, and then replied genially, "You're a cab, sir."†

---

*Cf. Bengt Ohrelius, Vasa: The King's Ship. *New York: Chilton Books, 1962.*

†*Choate, according to his family, later told the enraged diplomat, "If you'd been better looking, I would have called you a* hansom *cab."*

A Diplomatic Reception

The first European ever seen in Sikkim was Deputy Commissioner Campbell of Darjeeling. He toiled his way up in the time of the great-grandfather of the present Chogyal.*

Campbell's materialization in the audience room dismayed His Highness.

CHOGYAL (*to his vizier, the only English-speaking courtier*): Who are these extraordinary creatures with red faces and hair growing out of their cheeks? They look like monkeys!

VIZIER (*blandly, bowing to Deputy Commissioner Campbell*): His Highness bids you welcome. He expresses the hope that your journey was not unduly arduous.

*Who told me the story in 1968.

UNBALANCED DIETS

Walking Iron Mine Finally Collapses

TOBATA, JAPAN — A bet made several years ago finally caught up with 51-year-old Otoichi Kawakami last night.

Mr. Kawakami had convulsions and fainted in downtown Tobata. He was rushed to a hospital where surgeons removed from his stomach 13 safety razors complete with blades, 21 nails, a fountain pen, a pencil, 56 toothbrushes, 20 chopsticks, a piece of wire netting, and part of the ribs of an umbrella. He said he swallowed the assortment on a bet several years ago. — *United Press*

Walking iron mine

Rupture of the Deep

A group of city dignitaries staged a festivity to celebrate the joining of the two shafts of a tunnel under a river. The party, which Sir Robert Davis, an authority on diving, described to Jacques Cousteau, took place down in the tunnel.

The dignitaries cheerfully drank a quantity of champagne. It tasted flat: since the tunnel was under pressure, the carbon dioxide bubbles were held in solution.

When the city fathers were hoisted to the surface the carbon dioxide in their stomachs erupted. They blew up like bullfrogs and had to be lowered hastily back into the tunnel again.*

Higher Education

College students of the '50s and '60s enjoyed swallowing whole schools of goldfish. They also practiced crowding into telephone booths (the record was 31 in one booth) and they liked to destroy pianos. Two Delta Chi members tore one apart, passing the fragments through a 9-inch ring, in 4 minutes and 51 seconds at Wayne State University, Detroit.

*Cf. Jacques Cousteau, The Silent World. New York: Harper and Row, 1953.

Contretemps

Victorien Sardou, the French playwright and *salon* figure, knocked over his wine glass at a dinner party. The lady next to him sprinkled salt on the stain. Sardou tossed some over his shoulder to ward off ill fortune, straight into the eyes of a waiter who was about to serve him chicken. The man clutched his eyes and the platter crashed to the floor.

The family dog, rising from his post by the fire, attacked the fowl so greedily that he began to choke.

The son of the house jumped up to wrestle the bone out of the dog's throat. The dog savagely bit the son's finger. It had to be amputated.

Eating Democrats

Alferd Packer ate five prospectors whom he was guiding over a high Colorado plateau in 1874.

The judge who sentenced Packer to hang indignantly pointed out that "There was only six Democrats in all of Hinsdale County and you ate five of them."*

---

*The Department of Agriculture startled the official community by dedicating the cafeteria in its Washington building to Alferd Packer in 1977. The General Services Administration then removed the dedicatory plaque, accusing the Department of Agriculture of "bad taste."

HIGH LIFE

The Mould of Form

Beau Brummel kept a special man to make only the thumbs of his gloves.

Clubland

The Secretary of the Atheneum, London, relates that a noble member, exasperated by slow service in the dining-room, finally asked his waiter indignantly, 'Do you know who I am?'

The waiter, contemplating the member with sympathetic concern, replied, 'No, sir. But I shall make inquiries and inform you directly.'

Alien Porn

Madame de Maintenon, wife of Louis XIV, had herself bled twice a week so that she would not blush at the salacious tales recounted by her courtiers.

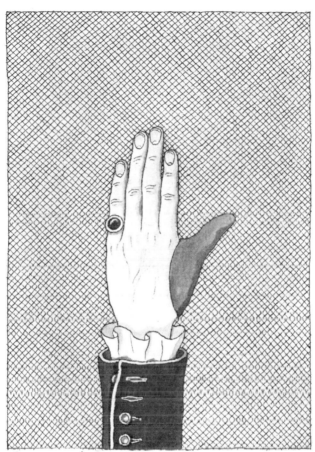

The mould of form

Trinkets

Trinkets

Moulay Ismael (Sultan of Morocco 1672–1727) used to send specimens of his bowel movements to court ladies as marks of special favor.*

Bobo Decides

"Lord Salisbury . . . asked me for the weekend to his country seat, Hatfield House. On a Friday afternoon I drew up before the ancient pile, built by Salisbury's ancestor, Sir Robert Cecil, first minister to Queen Elizabeth and James I.

"I paid off the taxi and timidly rang a doorbell. To my surprise, Lady Salisbury, a gray-haired lady with a strong ancestral face, answered the bell. With her was an enormous hound, which looked at me in a markedly unfriendly fashion and growled. . . .

"Lady Salisbury . . . saw that I was nervous. 'Don't worry,' she said. 'Bobo never bites a gentleman, only tradesmen and the lower classes.'

"At this point, Bobo lunged forward and planted his teeth in my right calf."†

*Visitors were impressed by his adroitness in mounting his horse. Sword in hand, he would leap into the saddle and simultaneously decapitate the slave who held his stirrup. It is estimated that he killed thirty thousand men with his own hand.

Cf. John Gunther, Inside Africa. New York: Harper & Row, 1955.
†Stewart Alsop, Stay of Execution. New York: J. B. Lippincott Company, 1973.

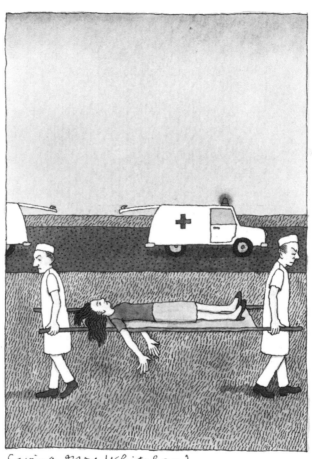

Saving Mrs Whitehead

MEDICINE

Saving Mrs. Whitehead

Mrs. Anna C. Whitehead of Nashville, Tennessee, was felled by a drunken driver, reported the *Nashville Tennessean* in January 1964. An ambulance was summoned from the Madison Funeral Home, but two other ambulances screamed first to the scene. The attendants leaped out and began to shout and struggle over the unconscious form, hauling it furiously back and forth while striking at one another. The police finally separated the combatants. Mrs. Whitehead was awarded to the original ambulance.*

*This strange scene recalls the tug-of-war at the funeral of Verlaine in 1896 between his publisher and his mistress over possession of the winding-sheet. (During which, incidentally, a second-rate figure called Louis Aï stole fourteen of the mourners' umbrellas that had been left leaning against a tree.)

Mars and Venus

"During the fray [May 12, between part of Grant's army and a Confederate detachment], a [soldier] staggered and fell to earth; at the same time a piercing cry was heard in the house near by. Examination of the wounded soldier showed that a bullet had passed through the scrotum and carried away the left testicle. The same bullet had apparently penetrated the left side of the abdomen of . . . [a] young lady midway between the umbilicus and the anterior spinous process of the ileum, and become lost in the abdomen. This daughter suffered an attack of peritonitis, but recovered. . . . Two hundred and seventy-eight days after the reception of the minié ball, she was delivered of a fine boy, weighing eight pounds, to the surprise of herself and the mortification of her parents and friends. . . . The doctor . . . concluded that . . . the same ball that had carried away the testicle of his young friend . . . had penetrated the ovary of the young lady, and, with some spermatazoa upon it, had impregnated her. With this conviction he approached the young man and told him the circumstances. The soldier appeared skeptical at first, but consented to visit the young mother; a friendship ensued which soon ripened into a happy marriage."*

*The American Weekly, *November 4, 1874; quoted in Gould and Pyle,* Anomalies and Curiosities of Medicine. *Philadelphia: The Julien Press, 1896.*

Ill Wind

When a cow has an attack of bloat (actually methane gas generated in the stomach) it must obtain relief promptly or it is likely to die.

A Dutch veterinarian was summoned recently to treat a cow suffering from this affliction, an agricultural news service reported. He tried a standard remedy, which is to insert a tube carefully up the beast's rear end.

A satisfying rush of gas followed.

With misplaced scientific zeal, the vet, perhaps seeking a source of cheap heat and light, then applied a match.

The resulting torchlike jet set the barn ablaze. It burned to the ground. The flames spread to the near by fields, which were consumed.

The vet was convicted of negligence and fined.

The cow remained serene.

A Difficult Patient

Ibsen himself spent the last six years of his life, unable to write, staring out of his window in Christiania.

One day when a nurse announced that he was feeling better, the old curmudgeon found the ultimate putdown. "On the contrary!" he said, and died.—*Time*, September 1971

Happy End

ATLANTA—Surgeons in Atlanta have successfully restored a severed penis to its owner, after it had been chopped off in a crime of passion. A 20-year-old man in rural South Carolina lost the organ to a butcher's knife wielded by his girl friend's estranged husband. Though it took six hours to get the victim to Atlanta's Emory University Hospital, the penis was put on ice and made the trip in satisfactory condition. Working for three hours, six Emory surgeons joined the organ's vein, two arteries and two nerves. When the victim went home a few weeks later, the penis was reportedly in full working order.* — *Moneysworth*

Diagnosis

The last words of Joseph Henry Green, the great English surgeon, were (pointing to his heart), "Congestion"; and then (taking his own pulse), "Stopped."

*The Washington Post *account added that the assailant had been indicted for "mayhem."*

SPORT

Hare Trigger

Near Louisville, Kentucky, a rabbit reached out of a hunter's game bag, pulled the trigger of his gun, and shot him in the foot. — *The New Yorker*, May 1947

Hunting Season Opens

ROME—Italy's hunting season began yesterday—with the hunters falling almost as fast as the pheasants.

The "bag" totaled at least nine people wounded and thousands more hurt in fighting over who had shot what.

The victims include two men who dropped dead in the excitement of the chase.

A hunter who fled is wanted for manslaughter and "failure to succour" a man he killed by mistake.

Another hunter was accidentally shot dead as he and a man argued over who had brought down a pheasant.

In the countryside outside Turin a grief-stricken

hunter turned his shotgun on himself after accidentally killing a man walking behind him, but two others overpowered him before he could pull the trigger.

Many of the stalking hunters were shot because they wore Alpine hats with plumes in them. The plumes were mistaken for pheasants. — London *Sun*

Mixed Bag

Lord Tennyson, in the 1850s, invited a Russian nobleman to his house on the Isle of Wight and used to send him off with a gun in the mornings to walk the hedgerows. One day the Russian came back looking pleased with himself and reported in a thick Slav accent that he had shot two peasants. Tennyson corrected him, saying "two pheasants." "No," said the Count, "two peasants. They were insolent, so I shot them."*

Royal Sport

The King of France and a party of 13 during an 18-day hunt in 1775, employing spears and hawks as well as guns, killed 47,950 head of game.

Jonathan Garnier Ruffer, The Big Shots—Edwardian Shooting Parties. *London: Debrett's Peerage Ltd., 1977.*

mixed bag

Sporting Print

Lord Charles Beresford* had an entire fox hunt—the Waterford hounds—tattooed in full cry on his back: hounds, horses, and riders, all in gorgeous color.

The fox, in this tableau, was just going to earth in the nearest hole, down which its brush was shown disappearing.

Dead Ducks

Dr. Ernest J. Fox, a veterinarian, of Georgetown, South Carolina, and his friend, Marshall Trueluck, went duck shooting at Annandale Plantation in 1976.

Two single birds, coming from opposite directions, whistled in to look at the decoys.

They cracked head on with great force. Both splashed into the water, stone dead.

Out of the Frying Pan

BY OUR SAO PAULO CORRESPONDENT—A man who went fishing on the banks of the Amazon's Rio Negro was attacked by infuriated bees after he struck their nest while trying to free his line from a tree.

To escape, he leapt into the river—and was devoured by piranhas.—London *Daily Telegraph*

"Charlie B." once telegraphed to decline an invitation: "So sorry can't come. Lie follows by post."

Cf. Geoffrey Bennett, Charlie B. *London: Peter Dawnay Ltd. 1968.*

Crossfire

Two gangsters, James Gallo and Joe Conigliaro, set about to murder a stool pigeon, Vinny Ensulo, alias Vinnie Ba Ba, alias Vincent Ennisie.

On November 1, 1973, they jumped him on Columbia Street, Brooklyn, and took him for a ride. Gallo pointed a gun at his head from the right, and Conigliaro covered him from the left. The car swerved violently. The two gangsters shot each other.*

Ms. Cooperman's Discomfiture

A woman named Cooperman recently went to court in New York to change her name to "Cooperperson."

Judge Scileppi denied the petition, on the grounds of "inanity."

---

*The New York Daily News *described the sequel. "Conigliaro, hit in the spine, was paralyzed. Every year after that Vinny Ensulo sent wheelchair batteries to Conigliaro. A small card with the batteries always said, 'Keep rolling, from your best pal, Vinny Ba Ba.'"*

Grit

During a motel holdup in Cleveland on May 3, 1977, the robber, Bruce Williams, was shot and paralyzed from the waist down.

He impressed the authorities the following year by committing five additional crimes within three months, including a robbery, a theft, and a kidnapping. The Associated Press in May 1978 quoted his comment on the work of the Cleveland police: "They pick on me," he said, from his wheelchair.

Cover-up

Of Pope John's trial at the Council of Constance in 1414-1418, Gibbon records that "The most scandalous charges were suppressed; the vicar of Christ was only accused of piracy, rape, murder, sodomy and incest."*

Wheeler-Peelers

GRAND RAPIDS, MICHIGAN — A local striptease joint must build ramps on its stage to accommodate handicapped strippers, state officials have ruled. — *Reuter*

This council was also attended by seven hundred harlots, according to reliable authorities — fifteen hundred, according to others.

Copulation

Copulation

Charlotte Oxford Tyler, mother of one, admitted during an investigation in Memphis in December 1973 to having had sex with several hundred policemen.*

Under questioning, she stated that this "may have had something to do with my belief in law and order."

Evidence

PHILADELPHIA—A former Philadelphia fireman, in Federal Court here trying to overturn his dismissal for long hair, set his head on fire.

"It must have been the hairspray I used," said the sheepish ex-fire-fighter, William Michini, who apparently tried to dramatize that his locks were not a safety threat to his job.

"Hair is self-extinguishing. It doesn't burn," he boasted.

With that he struck a match and held it to his head, which caught fire. — *Associated Press*

Together with 500 in the mid-South area, according to some press accounts. Asked about the inconveniences of sex in squad cars with officers wearing guns, truncheons, bullet belts, handcuffs, and angular badges, she replied, according to the Press-Scimitar, "It's just something you have to get used to working around."

That's baseball

That's Baseball

The Empress Eugénie staggered from the gory debris of her carriage after a bomb attack in which ten persons were killed and about 140 wounded.

"*C'est le métier,*"* she pronounced philosophically.

Traffic

In 1895 there were only two cars in the whole state of Ohio. They collided.

The Glory that Was Greece

L'Abbé Fourmont's innovation in classical travel was to obliterate the wonders of antiquity after he had inspected them.

"For the last month," he wrote in 1729, "thirty and sometimes forty or sixty workers have been smashing, destroying, *exterminating* the town of Sparta.

"This was the only way to make my trip a real hit (*rendre illustre mon voyage*). Imagine my joy if you can ... Sparta is the fifth city of the Morea that I have torn down . . . I did not reprieve Argos or Phylasia."

*"*It's all in the day's work.*"

The attempted assassination of Napoleon III and the Empress was carried out on January 14, 1858, outside the Opéra.

Cf. Harold Kurtz, The Empress Eugénie, 1826–1920. *Boston: Houghton Mifflin, 1964.*

The Zambian Space Program

Quite early in the space race Minister of Space Nkoloso of Zambia announced that his country would have a man on the moon by 1970.

After a while reporters were invited to witness one of the program's high points. An unfortunate individual was stuffed in a barrel, to which was fastened a rope looped around a stout tree. Strong assistants then whirled the barrel around and around the tree. It was explained that this experience would familiarize the man in the barrel with some of the problems of orbital flight.*

*In another phase of the program the future astronauts were rolled downhill in oil drums and trained to walk on their hands, said by the minister to be "the only way humans can walk on the moon."

1729

G. H. Hardy, the Cambridge mathematician, liked to describe his visit to Putney to call on the Indian mathematical prodigy Srinivasa Ramanujan, who was ill.

Hardy came in a cab with the number 1729. It was, he suggested, a dull number.

Ramanujan was indignant. "It is a very interesting number," he retorted. "It is expressible as the sum of two cubes in two different ways."*

The Dean's Humor

Jonathan Swift (author of *Gulliver's Travels*, and a clergyman) published a work under the *nom de plume* of Isaac Bickerstaff, entitled *Predictions for the Year 1708*. In it he foretold that a prominent figure he disliked, called John Partridge, editor of an almanac, would "infallibly die upon the 29th of March next."

On March 30, Swift, under a different pseudonym, published a confirmation that Partridge had indeed died.

The desperate victim struggled to refute this canard, but the public, including his readers, remained

* *They are $12^3 + 1^3$ and $10^3 + 9^3$.*

Cf. G. H. Hardy, Ramanujan. *Cambridge: Cambridge University Press, 1940.*

convinced that he was dead, and the new "Partridge" merely an impostor who hoped to take over the business.

As a result, his almanac had to suspend publication. Partridge never found out who had engineered the savage hoax.*

The Odd Guest

On a trip to Paris, the geographer Von Humboldt, after whom the Humboldt Current is named, asked an alienist friend (as psychiatrists were then called) if it would be possible to have dinner with a lunatic. The alienist was glad to oblige.

At dinner, one guest, of reserved manner, dressed in black with a white cravat, remained silent. The other, strangely attired and with his hair in disarray, babbled continuously with his mouth full.

During the fruit course Baron von Humboldt, discreetly indicating this curious figure, muttered to his host, "I like your lunatic . . . he amuses me."

"But it's the other one who's the lunatic!" whispered the alienist. "The man you're pointing at is Monsieur Honoré de Balzac!"

*Cf. Irwin Ehrenpris, Swift. New York: Methuen & Company, 1967.

the odd guest

BUSINESS

I. D.

NEW YORK—Sharon Mitchell, heroine of the X-rated *Captain Lust*, was having trouble cashing a check at a New York bank because she was not carrying a driver's license or any other identification.

She *was* carrying a magazine in which she appeared in the nude. She handed over the magazine, hitched her sweater up to her chin, and arranged herself in the same pose.

They cashed her check.*—*London* Sunday Telegraph Magazine

Anna Mingo, 18, a chambermaid of Teignmouth, England, manifested a similar pragmatism when she fell into a manhole. Thanks to her outstanding proportions (42-24-38), she stuck fast in the opening. "No doubt about it, my bust saved me," she announced happily to the press after she had been successfully extracted.

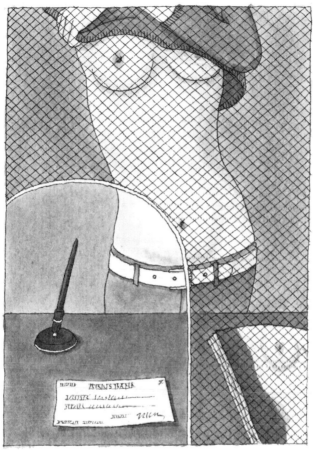

I.D.

A Deal's a Deal

In 1890 an indigent Swede sold the rights to his body after death to the Royal Swedish Institute of Anatomy. The seller became rich and twenty years later applied to buy back the contract. The institute turned him down. The seller went to court. The institute fought the suit and won.

The institute then applied to the court for compensation on the grounds that two teeth had been extracted from its property without its permission. The future cadaver was forced to pay damages.

Investigate Before You Invest

The result of a door-to-door survey of five thousand typical Americans was reported by *Collier's* in May 1949. Asked what was bought and sold on the New York Stock Exchange, 64 percent replied, "Livestock."

Hot Seat

When the electric chair first became popular, shortly before the turn of the century, Emperor Menelik II of Ethiopia, hearing of this marvel, ordered it from America. Alas, it didn't work.

No one had told the emperor that for best results one needed electricity. Ethiopia had none.

The Abyssinian underworld relaxed. Menelik ordered the chair fitted up as a throne, which he put into regular service.

IMBROGLIOS

Tumbling the Plumber

BELGRADE — A Belgrade plumber, Mr. Miodrag Jocic, who was called to attend to the sink in the home of a newly married couple, ended up in hospital with concussion and a broken leg.

The wife was out when Mr. Jocic arrived at the house. When she returned, she found a pair of legs sticking out from under the sink, and thought they belonged to her husband. Exactly what she did next is not certain, but it caused the plumber to bang his head into the sink above him.

The ambulance arrived to take him to hospital and while he was being carried down the stairs on a stretcher, one of the ambulance men asked him what had happened. On being told, he was so convulsed with laughter that he dropped the stretcher and the plumber tumbled down the stairs and broke a leg.

He is in hospital now, threatening to sue. The husband says that the incident so upset his wife that she will have nothing to do with him. —London *Times*

Plat du Jour

ZURICH — Hans and Erna W., who asked the mass circulation *Blick* newspaper not to print their full name, took their poodle Rosa along with them to an evening meal in Hong Kong.

They asked a waiter over to the table. After ordering, they pointed to the poodle while they made eating motions to show they wanted it to be fed.

Eventually the waiter took Rosa off into the kitchen. Later he came back with their main dish and when they picked up the silver lid they found their poodle roasted inside, garnished with pepper sauce and bamboo shoots.

The couple returned to Zurich immediately.
— *Reuter*

Fire Drill

PHILADELPHIA — The Lacey Park and Southampton volunteer fire departments set an abandoned rowhouse complex ablaze in Warminster Heights, Bucks County, Monday night so that they could practice putting it out.

By the time they did put the fire out, 150 residents of nearby buildings had had to be evacuated, the electricity of all Warminster Heights had been out for several hours, firemen had been called in from five neighboring communities and the Johnsville Naval

Plat du jour

Air Base, and there had been extensive smoke, heat, and water damage to nearby buildings and cars.

What the Lacey Park and Southampton firemen had discovered, just after setting the fire, was that they did not have any water.

"Boy, that was really dumb," said a Dean Street resident, Mrs. Roy Hopkins, who watched the blaze with her daughter.

"Yeah, it was dumb," agreed Mrs. Karen Zeno of the nearby Ashwood Apartments.*—Philadelphia *Inquirer*

Harassment

A conservatively dressed man who boarded the Seventh Avenue Subway at the Times Square station was the victim of a strange assault, reported by *The New York Times* in March 1969.

Firefighters in the West were also beset, as reported in the Washington Post *in February 1977.*

"For the last seven months, the National Park Service has been trying to put out a fire in a 25,000-year accumulation of giant sloth dung in a remote Grand Canyon cave."

"So far the agency has not succeeded, and the effort has cost $50,000. . . . Smithsonian Institution paleobiology curator Dr. Clayton Ray said . . . the Shasta sloth—which he does not like to call a giant sloth 'because he was only about the size of a black bear, nothing huge' — was not very notable except for producing a large and durable stool in the same place for about 25,000 years."

He was followed by a weird youth with frizzy hair who suddenly stuck his foot in the door, preventing the train from departing. Pointing his finger at the gentleman, he screamed over and over, "Give me back my yo-yo!"

The gentleman maintained a dignified silence.

Finally another passenger, announcing that he had to get to work, pushed the deranged youth's foot away, the doors closed, the train pulled out of the station.

Just below Thirty-fourth Street the gentleman reached into his coat pocket and, smiling enigmatically, began to spin a large, red yo-yo.

The Last Words of General Sedgwick

"Come, come!" said the general stoutly to some men who were dodging about under the enemy's fire.* "Why, they couldn't hit an elephant at this dist . . ."

*At Spotsylvania, May 9, 1864.

Cf. O. W. Holmes, Touched With Fire. Cambridge: Harvard University Press, 1947.

INDEX